P9-DGL-532

THE BUILDING BLOCKS OF BUSINESS WRITING

Jack Swenson

CRISP PUBLICATIONS, INC.
Los Altos, California

THE BUILDING BLOCKS OF BUSINESS WRITING

Jack Swenson

CREDITS
Editor: **Elaine Brett**
Design and Composition: **Interface Studio**
Cover Design: **Carol Harris**
Artwork: **Ralph Mapson**

All rights reserved. No part of this book may be reproduced or transmitted in any form or by any means now known or to be invented, electronic or mechanical, including photocopying, recording, or by any information storage or retrieval system without written permission from the author or publisher, except for the brief inclusion of quotations in a review.

Copyright © 1991 by Crisp Publications, Inc.
Printed in the United States of America

English language Crisp books are distributed worldwide. Our major international distributors include:

CANADA: Reid Publishing Ltd., Box 69559—109 Thomas St., Oakville, Ontario Canada L6J 7R4. TEL: (416) 842-4428, FAX: (416) 842-9327

AUSTRALIA: Career Builders, P. O. Box 1051, Springwood, Brisbane, Queensland, Australia 4127. TEL: 841-1061, FAX: 841-1580

NEW ZEALAND: Career Builders, P. O. Box 571, Manurewa, Auckland, New Zealand. TEL: 266-5276, FAX: 266-4152

JAPAN: Phoenix Associates Co., Mizuho Bldg. 2-12-2, Kami Osaki, Shinagawa-Ku, Tokyo 141, Japan. TEL: 3-443-7231, FAX: 3-443-7640

Selected Crisp titles are also available in other languages. Contact International Rights Manager Tim Polk at (415) 949-4888 for more information.

Library of Congress Catalog Card Number 90-84922
Swenson, Jack
The Building Blocks of Business Writing
ISBN 1-56052-095-7

ABOUT THIS BOOK

The Building Blocks of Business Writing is not like most books. It has a unique "self-paced" format that encourages a reader to become personally involved. Designed to be "read with a pencil," an abundance of exercises and activities invite participation.

The objective of *Building Blocks* is to present a practical procedure for building basic skills and improving letters and memos.

The Building Blocks of Business Writing (and the other books listed on page 72) is valuable in several ways. Here are some possibilities:

Individual Study. Because the book is self-instructional, all that is needed is a quiet place, some time, and a pencil. Completing the activities and exercises will provide practical steps for self-improvement.

Workshops and Seminars. This book is ideal as pre-assigned reading for a formal training session. With the basics in hand, more time can be spent on concept extensions and advanced applications. The book is also effective when used as part of a workshop or seminar.

Remote Location Training. Copies can be sent to those not able to attend "home office" training sessions. *Building Blocks* also makes an excellent desk reference book.

There are other possibilities that depend on the needs or objectives of the user. You are invited to find uses that will provide benefits for your program.

CONTENTS

CHAPTER 1—INTRODUCTION

A Simple Procedure

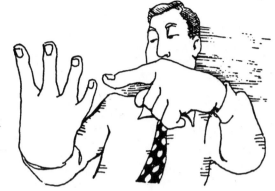

This is a book for people who want to improve their writing. This is also a book for people who are willing to work hard to achieve this goal. The ability to communicate in writing is a valuable skill. It can help you get the job you want, or get a better job. But nobody acquires language ability overnight. It takes study, thought, and practice to build writing skills. If you want to be a better writer, decide now to put some real effort into this project. This book will show you a simple, common-sense way to achieve your goal. It will help you improve your grammar usage, spelling skills, and writing style. The book explains a practical procedure for building basic skills and improving letters and memos. All that you need to get started is a pen or a pencil.

Learning to write well is simple. All it takes is commitment, time, and hard work! If you want to see improvement in your writing and if you want to get the most out of the suggestions and exercises in this book, you must do four things: *study*, *work*, *apply*, and *write*.

1. **Study the book.**

2. **Work through the exercises.**

3. **Apply the rules.**

4. **Write, write, write!**

Study the book. Don't just skim the instructions and suggestions that precede the exercises. Read carefully. Underline or highlight sentences that you want to remember and suggestions that seem especially useful. This allows you to review the material quickly later. If you're like most people, you may have to read something several times before it makes sense.

Work through all the exercises. Don't take any shortcuts. Do each exercise carefully. For your convenience, the answers for each exercise are provided in the book. You won't have to look in the back of the book or in a separate manual to find them—they're usually on the same page. It's very important not to skip any of the exercises. You may say to yourself, ''I use standard English; I don't have to do this one,'' or ''I'm a good speller; I think I'll skip this section and watch TV instead.'' Don't. Read the book from cover to cover and do every exercise.

Apply the suggestions and rules you learn to your own writing. Without this vital connection step, you may become good at doing exercises, but you will not become a good writer. Begin to pay closer attention to what you write and how you write it. Part of becoming a good writer is becoming a good editor. Don't worry about rules, about ''proper English,'' when you are writing. Just get your thoughts down on paper. When you have a first draft in hand, get out a pencil or pen and go over it. Check your work for grammatical correctness, spelling, punctuation errors, etc. **You may even be lucky enough to have a personal computer with a word processing package—this makes writing and then editing your work very easy.**

Write every day. Practice writing letters and memos. Do a brief report on some subject that interests you. You can use the written word for purposes other than communication. Put words down on paper to get ideas and problems clear in your mind; this process often helps to clear up confusion. The important thing is to *practice*. It helps to read books on writing and to take writing courses. But principles need to be applied. You learn how to write the same way you learn how to drive a car or mix cement. *All* skills are learned the same way. You make sure you understand the directions, and then you practice.

Start at the Beginning

Learning to write well is a three-stage process. One stage is learning the fundamentals: grammar, spelling, punctuation, and capitalization. Stage two is developing an effective writing style. Once you learn the fundamentals, you will want to move on to this second stage and learn how to send clear and expressive messages. You may work on the problem of wordiness, for example, or think about word choice—whether a simple word or a fancy one has the exact meaning you need. Stage three is the strategy stage. Here you perfect the skill of writing. When you are at this stage, you turn your attention to such matters as approach and format.

It is possible to work on all three stages at once. But beginning writers should start at the beginning. Do the things you need to do first before you worry about ''the finishing touches.'' Maybe you are not a beginning writer. Maybe you have been using the English language all your life, but for one reason or another, there are gaps in your knowledge. Maybe you are a pretty good speller, but your knowledge of proper grammar and punctuation rules is shaky. Or maybe your grammar usage is good, but you are a poor speller. In any case, a review of the fundamentals will be a helpful first step. This book is concerned primarily with the first stage, the fundamentals. By studying it and completing the exercises conscientiously, you will be building a base for further writing improvement.

Building the Foundation

Building writing skill is like building a house. The first job is to build a foundation. There are four ''building blocks'' that need to be in place before the construction of a writing project can continue. These building blocks are (1) grammar, (2) spelling, (3) punctuation, and (4) mechanics, which includes capitalization. These skills provide a firm foundation for clear and effective writing, and it is on these areas that this book concentrates.

Later in the book you will turn your attention to developing a pleasing writing style. In other words, once the foundation is in place, you can erect the wall framing, the beams, the rafters.

The last stage in building a house is doing the finish work. It's the same thing in building writing skill. When the foundation is in place and the frame and roof are up, the builder can turn his or her attention to the finishing touches. The last chapter of this book discusses some principles of writing strategy and shows you how to apply all you have learned in business memos and letters.

No Shortcuts

There are no shortcuts in this building project. You have to have a solid foundation or the floors will sag and the plaster will crack. Work hard on getting the foundation right to begin with. Grammar (Chapter 2) is especially important. In this world of computers and spelling checkers, you may be able to get by without being a good speller, but no software package has mastered grammar usage yet. You can't always depend on computers to fix your spelling, either— there are times when a word processor isn't handy. Misspelled words in a letter or memo are embarrassing, even professionally fatal. Study the chapter on spelling (Chapter 3). Even good spellers will find the tips and suggestions and introduction to spelling rules useful.

Another important building block is punctuation (Chapter 4). It's not necessary to learn *all* of the punctuation rules, but a few are essential. The final building block is mechanics (Chapter 5). Mechanics covers the capitalization rules—for example, whether it's correct to write "summer" or "Summer," "my mother" or "my Mother." (The first is correct in both cases, by the way.)

In addition to rules for using capital letters, this chapter also explains the proper use of quotation marks.

Getting Started

Are you ready to begin your building project? If so, get a pen or pencil and start working on Chapter 2. Work hard but have patience. It takes a while for some of the rules and principles to sink in. When you think you understand a rule or a pitfall to avoid, immediately apply this new knowledge to your own writing. Remember, *practice* is the way we learn how to do anything well.

CHAPTER 2—GRAMMAR

Express Yourself in Complete Sentences

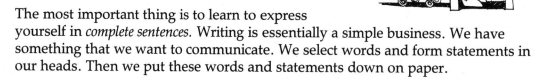

Good grammar is essential. Grammar is the first block in the foundation of language skills. The English grammar system is complicated and has many rules. Some rules are more important than others. In this book, we will concentrate on just a few of the most crucial principles.

The most important thing is to learn to express yourself in *complete sentences.* Writing is essentially a simple business. We have something that we want to communicate. We select words and form statements in our heads. Then we put these words and statements down on paper.

Most people can get thoughts down on paper clearly enough to be understood. But our goal as writers ought to be to communicate messages that are both clear and correct. A letter or memo with several errors in grammar does not make a good impression. Poor grammar often makes it difficult to understand the writer's meaning. It's annoying to have to ''translate'' a poorly written communication.

Think of writing, then, as simply putting your thoughts down on paper, one at a time. Begin by assembling the words in your mind. Put them in order. When you have a first sentence in your head, immediately get it down on paper or type it into your computer. Make it a complete thought, not random bits and pieces.

Incomplete:	Meeting in the manager's office next Wednesday. All staff assistants.
Complete:	There will be a meeting for all staff assistants in the manager's office next Wednesday.

When you have this sentence down, add sentences two, three, four, and so on. This process may sound slow and painful, but once you have the first sentence down, the others usually flow naturally and easily. Writing is merely a process of communicating information or ideas one sentence at a time.

What Is A Sentence?

Since messages are made up of sentences, you have to be sure that you know what a sentence is. Not every group of words with a period after it is a sentence. It may be an incomplete thought, or it may be two or more sentences strung together.

A sentence is a complete statement. It stands on its own. It may make a statement, ask a question, or give a command, but it is grammatically complete. It gives the reader all the information necessary to communicate a single thought.

Here's a suggestion that may help you without any further discussion or exercises. It's simply this: *train yourself to use short sentences.* If you will simply learn to use the period (.) more frequently, your problem with incomplete sentences or sentences strung together with commas (,) may all but disappear. **Keep it simple,** at least at first.

A good rule for business writers is to keep sentences shorter than 20 words. Short sentences mean clearer messages. Use common sense about this, of course. The length of your sentences should vary. If they are all the same length, your writing will seem mechanical and stiff. Also, if all your sentences are very short, your writing will seem childlike. But as a rule, use short sentences. This will help you remember to express your thoughts in complete statements.

Recognizing Incomplete Sentences

The next step is to learn to *recognize* incomplete and run-together sentences. You have to learn to tell sentences from groups of words that *look* like sentences but are not.

First, let's compare a sentence with a group of words that is not a sentence. Which of these two groups of words is a sentence?

1. Because I was sick yesterday.

2. I missed some work due to illness.

If you said that number two is a sentence, you're right. Compare the two groups of words. You should notice one thing immediately. The second example makes a complete statement, the first does not. Information is missing from number one. It leaves the reader hanging, waiting for the thought to be completed.

Something else is different about the two examples. The first example begins with the word "because," which is called a *dependent word*. When a dependent word begins a phrase, it makes the phrase dependent on another thought. Without that thought, the sentence is incomplete. A complete sentence containing the words in number one could be: "I missed the meeting because I was sick yesterday." The dependent thought is now completed.

A good way to learn to recognize incomplete sentences is to watch out for dependent words. It's okay to use these words in sentences. But when they begin statements, watch out for incomplete thoughts. Here is a list of dependent words:

Dependent Words		
after	since	whereas
although	so that	wherever
as	than	whether
as if	that	which
because	though	whichever
before	unless	while
even if	until	who
even though	what	whom
ever since	whatever	whose
how	when	why
if	whenever	
in order that	where	

EXERCISES AHEAD

In the following exercise, see if you can tell the good sentences from the faulty ones. Is the complete sentence in each pair A or B? Pick out the complete sentences and mark the letter in the blank.

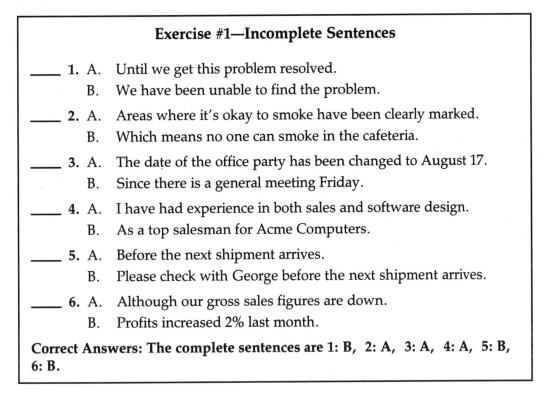

Exercise #1—Incomplete Sentences

_____ 1. A. Until we get this problem resolved.
B. We have been unable to find the problem.

_____ 2. A. Areas where it's okay to smoke have been clearly marked.
B. Which means no one can smoke in the cafeteria.

_____ 3. A. The date of the office party has been changed to August 17.
B. Since there is a general meeting Friday.

_____ 4. A. I have had experience in both sales and software design.
B. As a top salesman for Acme Computers.

_____ 5. A. Before the next shipment arrives.
B. Please check with George before the next shipment arrives.

_____ 6. A. Although our gross sales figures are down.
B. Profits increased 2% last month.

Correct Answers: The complete sentences are 1: B, 2: A, 3: A, 4: A, 5: B, 6: B.

Not all incomplete sentences begin with dependent words, but many of them do. If you answered most of the questions correctly in the above exercise, you are well on your way to solving the problem of writing incomplete sentences. Look for such sentences in your own writing.

Run-Together Sentences

Now let's look at another problem. In a way, this problem is the opposite of the one we just discussed. Sometimes the trouble is not incomplete sentences, but rather two or more complete sentences that are run together without punctuation or with improper punctuation.

Remember that a period is used to mark the end of a sentence. Which of the following is the properly punctuated sentence?

A. Congratulations to Bill Harper, who exceeded his sales quota by 16%.

B. Bill Harper is currently our top salesman he should be congratulated.

C. All the salesmen made a real effort, everybody worked hard all month.

The correct answer is A. B needs a period after the word ''salesman,'' and the comma in C should be changed to a period. In the following exercise, add necessary periods. Place a period after each complete sentence. *Note:* Some of the sentences may be complete already. Do not add periods to these sentences.

Exercise #2—Run-Together Sentences

1. I would like to have my hours changed I cannot work Wednesday evening because of a family commitment.

2. Thank you for your letter I'm really happy that you are pleased with our product.

3. We need to do something about the problem of poor ventilation in the stockroom.

4. The company softball team won again Friday Jim ''Nolan Ryan'' Kennedy struck out 17 batters.

5. The report will be ready Monday I'm sure that it will provide the information you need.

6. I enjoy working with people I've had two years of experience on the order desk I'm also currently attending a junior college to further my education.

Correct Answers: 1. changed. I cannot... 2. letter. I'm... 3. (Okay) 4. Friday. Jim... 5. Monday. I'm sure... 6. people. I've... desk. I'm also...

In the following exercise, the writer has made an attempt to separate sentences, but the sentences are improperly linked with commas. Change the incorrectly used commas to periods. *Note:* Commas may be used *within* sentences. In the examples that follow, some commas are correct. Change only those commas that incorrectly separate complete sentences.

Exercise #3—Run-Together Sentences

1. As a result, we cannot complete your order at this time, we will forward the missing items when they are shipped.

2. I have enjoyed working for Smith & Company, I have learned a lot these past two years.

3. I have been happy here, but I feel that it is time to move on, I plan to go back to school to further my education and then begin a career in communications.

4. I want the job very much, I understand that Nordquist's has a very good management training program.

5. I need a day off to take care of personal business, I will make up the time, of course, by working extra hours next week.

6. In my opinion, the new ''no smoking'' rules are unfair, people who choose to smoke have rights, too.

**Correct Answers: 1. time. We...   2. Company. I have...   3. on. I plan...
4. much. I...   5. business. I will...   6. unfair. People...**

Fixing Faulty Sentences

Now for the final step. How can we correct incomplete or run-together sentences? You have already done some repair work in the exercises above, so you may be able to answer this question yourself. What you have learned, plus common sense, may tell you what needs to be done. But let's go over the problem one more time, just to make sure.

Incomplete sentences are not really sentences. They may look like sentences because they begin with a capital letter and end with a period, but they are not complete statements. Many incomplete sentences can be fixed by simply **attaching** them to the previous sentence or the sentence that comes next.

Incomplete:	*Because my car wouldn't start.* I was late for work Monday.
Complete:	Because my car wouldn't start, I was late for work Monday.

We can arrange the words in a complete sentence in several ways. We can put a dependent phrase either at the beginning or the end of the sentence, for example.

Correct:	Because my car wouldn't start, I was late for work Monday.
Correct:	I was late for work Monday because my car wouldn't start.

Both of these sentences are correct. Notice that if the dependent phrase (beginning with the dependent word "because") begins the sentence, a comma is placed between the dependent phrase and the main sentence. If the dependent phrase is placed at the *end* of the sentence, the comma is omitted.

A second way to repair an incomplete sentence and to make it a complete thought is by **adding words**.

Incomplete:	The staff will have to work overtime next week. *Whether they like it or not.*
Complete:	The staff will have to work overtime next week. *They will have to do this* whether they like it or not.

Sometimes incomplete sentences do not begin with a dependent word. We can usually repair such sentences by adding a few words.

Incomplete:	I am enclosing the information you requested. *Glad to be of service.*
Complete:	I am enclosing the information you requested. *We are* glad to be of service.

Now let's see if you can fix some faulty sentences. In the following exercise, either **attach** the incomplete sentence to another sentence or **add words** to the faulty sentence to make it complete. *Note:* Some sentences may be correct and require no changes. Also, when you compare your answers to the correct answers at the end of the exercise, you may have added words that differ from the words used in the suggested correction. This is not important. The words may vary; what's important is making the sentence complete.

Exercise #4—Incomplete Sentences

1. Jim works hard and is always on time. A good employee.
2. Because I know that I need more education for advancement. I have signed up for two college classes next semester.
3. Before I agree to the transfer. I would like you to explain in detail my new responsibilities.
4. This will have to be a team effort. Because the Bemis account is very important to the company.
5. The company appreciates your extra effort. Thanks for working this weekend to put in the hours that were necessary to complete the job.
6. Off to Hawaii! I hope the boys in the stockroom can get along without me during the next two weeks.

Correct Answers: 1. time. He is a good... 2. advancement, I have...
3. transfer, I would... 4. effort because 5. (Okay) 6. I'm off...

14

You have learned that one of the ways to correct an incomplete sentence is to change a period to a comma. The opposite is true for run-together sentences. To repair this common writing error, place a period at the end of the sentence, in some cases replacing a comma. Identify complete statements in your writing, and be sure each statement ends with a period.

In the following exercise, place a period at the end of every sentence. If there is no punctuation, simply add a period. If a comma has been incorrectly placed at the end of the sentence, change the comma to a period. Some of the sentences may be correct as they are. Do not change these sentences. Remember that it is correct to use commas *within* sentences. Only replace the commas that are incorrectly placed at the end of sentences.

Exercise #5—Run-Together Sentences

1. Thank you for your letter informing us about the billing error we will correct the mistake immediately.

2. Say hello to Mary and Lois for me, it was a pleasure to work with them on the project last month.

3. On the other hand, we may not need the extra help, I'll have to clear it with Mr. Watson, but he is on vacation this week.

4. This is to inform you that we have completed our inspection, everything checks out, and it is okay for you to go ahead.

5. Volunteers are needed to clean up after the Christmas party please tell Jan if you are willing to help.

6. Unfortunately, I have misplaced the order, but if you will send me a copy or write out a new order, I will ship the merchandise immediately.

**Correct Answers: 1. error. We will...   2. me. It was...   3. help. I'll...
4. inspection. Everything...   5. party. Please...   6. (Okay)**

The easiest way to correct run-together sentences is to place a period at the end of each complete statement. However, there are other remedies. Instead of separating statements with a period, you can use a semicolon (;).

Incorrect: We cannot fill your order__we are returning your check.

Incorrect: We cannot fill your order, we are returning your check.

Correct: We cannot fill your order. We are returning your check.

Correct: We cannot fill your order; we are returning your check.

OR

We cannot fill your order; therefore we are returning your check.

A third way to fix run-together sentences is by connecting sentences with a linking word plus a comma. The linking words are and, but, or, nor, for, and sometimes so and yet.

Correct: We cannot fill your order, so we are returning your check.

Which is the best way to correct a run-together sentence? Use a period. Keep it simple.

16

Review

Let's review what you have learned about sentences so far.

1. **Write in complete sentences.**

2. **A sentence makes a complete statement.**

3. **Use short sentences.**

4. **Watch for dependent words.**

5. **Watch for commas that incorrectly link two sentences.**

6. **Fix incomplete sentences by attaching them to complete sentences or by adding words.**

7. **Fix run-together sentences by adding periods or changing commas to periods.**

Now, test your knowledge of sentences by correcting the mistakes in the memo in the next exercise. You will find both incomplete and run-together sentences.

Exercise #6—Incomplete and Run-Together Sentences

to <u>All Staff</u>   from Joyce Bendorf
subject <u>Liz Hanada</u>   date <u>October 4, 1990</u>

1 Many of you have inquired as to Liz Hanada's present state of health, she was readmitted to Logan Hospital about a month ago. With seriously low blood counts that required four units of blood transfusions. A number of medical tests were performed to find the source of the problem. After five days in the hospital, Liz stayed with her family in Portland to recuperate.

2 Liz's blood levels are being maintained through blood transfusions. She especially wanted to thank Bill Cardenas, Margie Johnson, Ben Harris, and Marie Hicks for coming to her rescue with blood donations. In her most recent crisis. She would also like to thank the Bidwell staff who donate to Bidwell's blood bank account. Which will assure that any of Liz's future needs for blood can be met.

3 It's been a year since Liz worked here at Bidwell Plastics she has missed all of you and appreciates your concern and support.

Correct Answers: 1. health. She / month ago with   2. donations in / account, which   3. Plastics. She

Now you know how to recognize and fix incomplete and run-together sentences. Be sure to **apply** this knowledge next time you write. The discussion and exercises will do you no good unless you make the effort to put what you have learned into practice.

This holds true for the grammar problems that we are going to turn our attention to next. Become an editor as well as a writer! Study the book. Then, the next time you write a letter or memo, go back over it looking for similar errors and make the necessary corrections.

Common Grammar Errors

In this section, you will learn to spot nine common grammar errors. You may not make all of these errors. For example, you may not have trouble with articles and prepositions or using nonstandard verbs. Study the material anyway. These nine errors are the ones found most frequently in the work of inexperienced writers.

1 Omitting Verb Endings

Do you know what a verb is? Prove it! Underline the verb in the following sentence.

The speeding car passed us on the freeway.

If you underlined the word ''passed,'' you correctly selected the verb. Verbs are the words in sentences that name actions. They tell what the subject of the sentence does or is. Verbs and nouns (words that name people, places, and things) are the most important words in a sentence. They carry a lot of responsibility. They do most of the work in communicating the writer's message.

Verbs have several forms. We may say ''I pass'' or ''I passed,'' for example. Or we may say ''I walk,'' ''I walked,'' or ''I have walked.'' What determines the form of the verbs we use is *when* the action happened—whether it's something going on now or something that occurred in the past. A common mistake beginning writers make is to leave off the ending of the verb, usually the letters <u>d</u> or <u>ed</u>, when describing past or completed action. Watch for such omissions in your own writing.

> **Wrong:** I report the problem to Mr. Shaw last Friday.
>
> **Right:** I report<u>ed</u> the problem to Mr. Shaw last Friday.

Watch also for omitted <u>s</u> endings. When the subject of the sentence is he, she, or it (or a singular noun that names some person other than the writer), use the s-form of the verb.

> **Wrong:** She cheerfully accept each new assignment.
>
> **Right:** She cheerfully accept<u>s</u> each new assignment.

2 Shifts in Time

Verb "tense" is a term that refers to the time of the action. Actions may occur in the present or be continuing actions or they may have occurred previously. Don't mix verb forms in a sentence. Stick to past or present time, whichever is appropriate.

> **Wrong:** He <u>call</u> the meeting for 9 A.M., and we <u>were</u> all there on time.
>
> **Right:** He <u>called</u> the meeting for 9 A.M., and we <u>were</u> all there on time.

3 Missing Articles

Articles are little words that come before nouns. In English, there are three articles: <u>a</u>, <u>an</u>, and <u>the</u>. A and an are used before nouns that name only one person, place or thing. <u>The</u> may be used before nouns that name one or more than one.

The main rule to remember about articles is that we use <u>an</u> before words that begin with vowels (a,e,i,o,u,), and <u>a</u> before words that begin with all the other letters in the alphabet. We say "an <u>egg</u>" but "a <u>typewriter</u>." This is a simple rule, but it can get a little tricky if the first letter of the word is <u>u</u> or if it is a silent letter. For example, we say "a <u>unit</u>" but "an <u>underlying</u> cause." It depends upon how the letter <u>u</u> is pronounced. If it's pronounced "uh," we use the article <u>an</u>. If it's pronounced "you," we use <u>a</u>.

Silent letters can also cause a problem. We say "an <u>h</u>onest man" because the letter <u>h</u> is silent, so the next letter (<u>o</u>) is the one that tells us which article to use.

The most common problem with articles for beginning writers is leaving these little words out. This is especially true of writers whose native language is not English. Not all languages have articles. English does. Don't omit articles.

Wrong:	I need typewriter because supervisor requires me to do daily reports.
Right:	I need <u>a</u> typewriter because <u>the</u> supervisor requires me to do daily reports.

In the following exercise, add missing verb endings and articles and change the form of the verb if the time (tense) is incorrect. You will find one or more errors in each of the sentences.

Exercise #7—Common Errors

1. The supervisor call a meeting Tuesday and tells the staff about the new inventory procedure.

2. We are having trouble with phone system; the voice mail feature did not seem to be working properly.

3. Richard has decide to quit and move to Chicago.

4. I work hard to find and correct every error; I wanted resume to be perfect.

5. All salesmen are require to turn in their expense reports by end of month.

6. We attended the morning workshop, and in the afternoon we have small group discussions.

Correct Answers: 1. called...told   2. the phone system...does not seem   3. decided   4. worked...the resume   5. required...the end of the month   6. we had small

---

4 Wrong Prepositions

Nonnative speakers of English, as well as some native speakers, may have trouble with prepositions. Like articles, prepositions are little words that come before nouns and pronouns in a sentence. Words such as <u>to</u>, <u>on</u>, <u>above</u>, <u>in</u>, and <u>from</u> are prepositions. Their purpose is to give more information about other words in the sentence. For example, we might tell where something is by saying it is "<u>in</u> the stockroom" or "<u>near</u> the stockroom."

A common problem with prepositions, especially for nonnative speakers, is using the wrong word. The writer uses <u>of</u> when he or she should use <u>at</u>, for example.

I was educated <u>of</u> a college in Tokyo, Japan.

Choose your words carefully. When you edit your letters and memos, watch for wrong words.

5 Errors in Agreement

Subjects, verbs, and pronouns should all "agree" (correspond grammatically) within a sentence. Subjects are nouns or pronouns that name the doer of an action described in the sentence. Verbs name the action. If the subject is singular, the verb should be singular. If the subject is plural, the verb should be plural.

Bill <u>has</u> his own office now.

Each of the salesmen <u>has</u> his own office.

In the sentences above, the subjects are "Bill" and "each." (In the second sentence, the word "salesmen" is part of the phrase "of the salesmen" and is not the subject.) Because both subjects are singular, the singular form of the verb is used. The singular verb is "has."

If the subject is plural, the plural form of the verb should be used.

Bill and Fred <u>have</u> their own offices now.

Trouble sometimes occurs because some speakers and writers do not know which words are singular and which are plural. Here is a list of words that are singular. When these words are used as subjects in a sentence, the verbs used with them should be singular.

anyone	nobody
everyone	somebody
one	each
someone	either
anybody	neither
everybody	

Here are some word pairs that you can always be sure are in agreement. There are no exceptions.

you were	(never ''you was'')
we were	(never ''we was'')
they were	(never ''they was'')
he doesn't	(never ''he don't'')
she doesn't	(never ''she don't'')
it doesn't	(never ''it don't'')

Similarly, a pronoun should also agree with the word it refers to. Pronouns are words that take the place of nouns to give a sentence variety. We could say, ''Mary answers the telephone, and Mary also types a letter occasionally.'' Instead, we are more likely to say, ''Mary answers the telephone, and she also types a letter occasionally.'' If the word referred to is singular, the pronoun should also be singular. In the sentence above, since the word referred to (Mary) names just one person, we must use a singular pronoun (she).

Refer to the list above to guide you in deciding which words are singular and which are plural. If the word referred to is singular, be sure the pronoun is also singular.

The following sentence is grammatically correct, but it has a different agreement problem.

Each of the salesmen has his own office.

What if some of the people on the sales force are women? Try to avoid sex bias in your writing. If you are sure the word referred to includes just men, it's okay to use ''his'' and ''salesmen.'' If you aren't sure, say ''his or her.'' Better yet, rewrite the sentence.

> **Wrong:** If anyone wants a ride, <u>he</u> can go in my car.
>
> **Right:** If anyone wants a ride, <u>he or she</u> can go in my car.
>
> **Right:** Anyone who wants a ride can go in my car.

6 Unclear Reference

Writers can't assume that because they know who or what they are referring to in a sentence, the reader will know, too. What does this sentence mean?

Sally told Linda that she would have to work Saturday.

Who is going to have to work Saturday, Sally or Linda? Probably Linda is going to have to put in the overtime, but the way the sentence is written, the pronoun "she" could refer to either Sally or Linda.

When you revise your writing, check carefully for pronouns that do not refer clearly to their subjects. Rewrite the sentence if there is some doubt in your mind.

> **Right:** Sally told Linda to come to work Saturday.
>
> **Right:** Sally said to Linda, "You are going to have to work Saturday."

In the following exercise, correct errors in word choice. Look for wrong prepositions, agreement errors, and unclear references for pronouns. You may find more than one error in some sentences. *Note:* If you rewrite a sentence, your answer may differ somewhat from the suggested correction given in the answer key that follows the exercise.

Exercise #8—Common Errors

1. A weight is attached with each end of the beam.
2. Every one of the employees give their best effort.
3. I've always been interested in programming and finally decided to become one.
4. Everybody expect her to be the next partner.
5. Either of the candidates are a good choice for the job.
6. The report was written with ink.

Correct Answers: 1. at each end   2. gave his or her best (or: The employees all gave their...)   3. decided to become a programmer.   4. expects   5. is a good choice   6. in ink

---

"Phrase" and "clause" are names for two kinds of groups of words. A clause has a subject and a verb and can form a sentence by itself. A phrase has no subject and verb and cannot form a complete sentence. It is a group of words that gives information about other words in a sentence.

Phrases need to be positioned logically in a sentence or the sentence will be unclear. Sometimes a misplaced phrase gives the reader a laugh at the writer's expense.

> At the age of three my family moved to Salinas, California.

The writer of this sentence has a very young family! To avoid such embarrassing sentences, try to position a phrase as close as possible to the word that it gives information about.

> When I was three years old, my family moved to Salinas, California.

8 Awkward Lists

When you list items in a sentence, be sure that the words or phrases are similar in structure. Avoid awkward mixes of words. Here are some examples.

> Kevin is good at filing, typing, and he knows how to keep books, too.

> She liked to work hard, to save her money, and then she would spend it all on a trip.

To fix the first sentence, use words that name office skills for all of the items on the list.

> Kevin is good at filing, typing, and bookkeeping.

To fix the second sentence, begin each item with the word "to."

> She liked to work hard, to save her money, and then to spend it all on a trip.

9 Nonstandard Words

Writers sometimes have writing problems because they do not know the standard forms of words. "Standard" means commonly accepted as good grammar in speaking and writing. Verbs cause most of the trouble. At least half of the errors made by beginning writers are verb errors. Can you correct the verb errors in the following sentences? The verbs are underlined.

Mr. Jones <u>travel</u> to Chicago two times a year.

Yesterday we <u>seen</u> a video on communication skills.

It <u>costed</u> us $109 to repair the answering machine.

The correct verbs should be "travels," "saw," and "cost."

Some writers have a problem knowing when and when not to add the letter <u>s</u> to a verb. To see if this is a problem for you, take the following test. Underline the correct verb form in each sentence.

I walk/walks to work.

He walk/walks to work.

All the employees walk/walks to work.

The correct answers are "walk," "walks," "walk."

For some, major problems are caused by the verbs <u>have</u>, <u>do</u>, and <u>don't</u>. The mistakes in the sentences below are typical.

Maureen <u>have</u> trouble getting to work on time.

We don't know yet who <u>done</u> it.

The correct verbs are "has" and "did."

Here is a chart that will help you if you frequently misuse these troublesome verbs.

I, you, we, they <u>have</u>
he, she, it <u>has</u>
I, you, we, they, he, she, it <u>had</u>
Mr. Jones <u>has</u> or <u>had</u>

I, you, we, they <u>do</u>
he, she, it <u>does</u>
I, you, we, they, he, she, it <u>did</u>
Mr. Jones <u>does</u> or <u>did</u>

I, you, we, they <u>don't</u>
he, she, it <u>doesn't</u>
I, you, we, they, he, she, it <u>didn't</u>
Mr. Jones <u>doesn't</u> or <u>didn't</u>

Another troublesome word is the verb "to be." This verb has several forms. The table below lists the proper forms.

I am	I was
you, we, they are	you, we, they were
he, she, it is	he, she, it was

Finally, don't confuse the verbs "lie" and "lay." Lie means to recline or rest on a surface and lay means to put or place something somewhere.

> **Wrong:** I had to lay down because I became dizzy.
>
> **Wrong:** She said she had lain the report on my desk Monday.

The correct verbs in these sentences are "lie" and "laid."

Verbs aren't the only troublemakers, of course. Beginning writers, or speakers of a dialect (a regional variety of English) may make other mistakes in word choice. Test your knowledge of standard English by finding and correcting the errors in the following sentences.

1. We didn't do nothing wrong.
2. I was going to be in the main office Wednesday anyways.
3. The foreman was not hisself today.
4. Carol tries awful hard.
5. The bookkeeper must of made an error.
6. If us secretaries band together, we can get management to see our point of view.

Correct Answers: 1. do anything   2. anyway   3. not himself   4. awfully 5. must have   6. we secretaries

In the exercise below, find and correct misplaced phrases, awkward lists, and wrong words. You may find more than one error in each sentence.

Exercise #9—Common Errors

1. The boss asked Les if he had did the report.

2. Each employee was given the choice of coming in early, working late, or they could come in Saturday.

3. Because of going to too many meetings, my report was late.

4. The guard had apparently fell asleep on the job.

5. We should of been more careful with Acme's order.

6. The regional manager don't visit us no more.

Correct Answers: 1. he had done   2. or coming in Saturday.   3. My report was late because I had to go to too many meetings.   4. fallen asleep 5. should have been   6. doesn't visit us anymore.

Now test your knowledge of the nine common grammar errors discussed in this chapter. Carefully read the letter in the exercise that follows. There are 10 errors. Find and correct each error.

Exercise #10—Common Errors

Dear Investor:

1 It's likely that many of your goals has been shaped by the traditions of your parents...and their parents. Perhaps their tradition of saving is one that you have carried on.

2 Today, you have added savings and investment choices to build for the future. And one very important part of your investment picture may be Acme Money Market Fund, investment that meets the traditional benefits of stability, liquidity, and impressive high yields, while also meeting today's demand for added safety.

3 In addition to high current yields, the Acme Money Market Fund seeks to maximize safety. By investing in short-term obligations issue by the U.S. government and their agencies—some of which is even backed by the full faith and credit of the U.S. government—and repurchase agreements backed by these securities, this fund offers investors an extra margin of safety.

4 Also, the fund is managed to maintain a stable $1 share price, so it should not fluctuate with changing market conditions.

5 Acme Money Market Fund offers you today's highest money market yields. All other things being equal, lower expenses can mean higher yields. And higher yields can bring you closer to fulfilling your savings objectives.

6 In order to achieve and retain high yields, a fund must commit to low costs. And that's exactly what Acme does. We guarantees that Acme Money Market Fund's operating expenses will never exceed 0.50%, all the way through 1992! That's substantially below the average operating expenses of other money market funds.

7 Plus, with Acme, you pay only for the transactions you makes. You don't have to share expenses incurred for the transaction on fellow shareholders. What's more, you pay no sales charge, so 100% of your money went to work for you seeking the highest possible current money market yields.

8 Put Acme's experience to work for your future. Today, more than 200,000 Acme shareholders depend on us to help make their financial goals a reality.

Correct Answers: 1. have been shaped   2. an investment that meets 3. obligations issued, its agencies, which are even backed   4. so your share price should not fluctuate   5. okay   6. We guarantee   7. you make, of fellow shareholders, money goes to work   8. okay

Standard English and Dialects

There are many varieties of English. Listen to people talk; you will hear many differences. Some say, "Hand me that bucket." Others say, "Get the pail." In Texas, the word "beer" is pronounced to sound like "bear." ("Git me another Lone Star bear.") When Easterners pronounce the name of the country's largest city, it comes out something like "Noo Yawk."

There are differences in grammar, too. A speaker of standard English would say, "He doesn't have his own office." Someone else might say, "He don't have his own office." Standard English is the variety of the language that is commonly accepted as correct.

We call these language variations dialects. All of these varieties of English enrich the language. They are colorful and interesting. But problems arise, for both speakers and writers, when they try to communicate in non-standard English with other people who speak a different variety of the language or who do use standard English. For example, speakers with a regional or foreign accent may find their listeners more interested in the *way* they speak than in their message. This is a handicap for salespeople and company representatives. People who are aware of this problem often take "accent reduction" classes in their spare time.

Writers have an even bigger problem. Readers expect standard English in letters, memos, and reports. They may be irritated or offended by nonstandard grammar and think poorly of the writer as a result.

The terms we use and the way we pronounce words are determined by where we live. Differences in grammatical usage are more likely to depend on culture and education. Writers who use nonstandard grammar can, with hard work, learn to use the standard forms. Here are some things that you can do to increase your knowledge of standard English.

1. Study the grammar chapter in this book, especially the sections on agreement and nonstandard words.

2. Look up words in the dictionary. The dictionary will tell you whether a word is standard or slang. It will also list the proper forms of verbs.

3. Take a grammar class. Most community colleges offer such classes.

4. Listen carefully and read widely. Take the time to notice how educated speakers and writers use the language.

Special Problems of Nonnative Speakers

If English is not your native language, you may have special problems. The English grammar system has many rules; learning these rules can be difficult and frustrating. Verbs cause the most trouble. Verbs have many forms. ''Drink'' is the right word sometimes. But other times we have to say ''drank'' or ''drunk.'' For some new Americans, articles and prepositions also cause trouble. Not all languages have articles. And the use of prepositions seems to be determined by custom.

There are no easy usage rules to guide the new English speaker and writer. The best advice is to study hard, listen carefully, and read widely. In time, it will come. Have patience!

Here are some suggestions that may help nonnative speakers solve the puzzle of English grammar.

1. Take a grammar class.

2. Ask a teacher or librarian to suggest a helpful grammar handbook or workbook.

3. Listen carefully to the speech of native speakers. Read English newspapers, magazines, and books. Set aside some time each day for reading.

4. Study the sections in this book which apply to your special language problems, especially the sections on omitted verb endings, articles, prepositions, and nonstandard grammar.

5. Choose your words carefully when you write. *Use* new words and forms of words that you learn. You won't learn to use the language properly unless you apply what you learn in your own writing.

All readers of this book should keep in mind the need for practical application. Study the book. Learn the rules. Watch for errors. When you write, get your thoughts down on paper, a sentence at a time. Then go back over what you have written and correct your mistakes. **Apply** what you have learned!

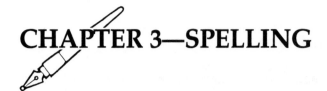

CHAPTER 3—SPELLING

Let the Computer Do It?

You have to build a solid foundation before you can build a house. The same thing is true of language skills. Work on the basics first. Spelling is a very important basic skill.

Why do you need to worry about spelling? After all, this is the 1990s. Everybody has a personal computer with a word processor that includes a spelling checker. Why not let computers handle the spelling mistakes we make?

For one thing, not everybody has a word processor or knows how to use one. Also, spelling checkers can help you with only certain kinds of words. By all means, use a spelling checker if it helps you. But recognize its limitations.

Using the spelling checker has several disadvantages:

1. It is time-consuming.

2. It cannot help you with the spelling of proper names unless you program it to do so.

3. It cannot tell you when you have confused similar words such as ''their'' and ''there.''

4. It lulls the user into thinking he or she has edited a letter or memo once the computer has done its job.

Perhaps the two problems listed last are the most serious. Do not assume that your proofreading task is over once you have allowed the machine to find spelling errors and you have corrected them. Be sure to reread your work carefully. Correct other errors as well. Many executives and managers say that their employees' writing is still lacking in correctness and attention to detail, even though they write using word processors.

Also, machines can't tell you if certain kinds of words are wrong. You may have written ''complement,'' for example, but meant ''compliment.'' To the machine, both words are correct. You can only tell which is the proper word by reading the sentence in which it appears. This has to be done by a person; a computer can't do it.

Commonly Confused Words

There are hundreds of these commonly confused words in English. We are going to concentrate on this problem first. Study the word pairs (and trios) that are listed and defined in this chapter. Notice the differences in spelling. Memorize the meanings.

Here are some words you must know:

1. **to, too, two**

    To means *toward, until;* it is also used before a verb.
    to the barn, five minutes to six, to sing

    Too means *more than enough* or *also.*
    He's too short. I want to go, too.

    Two means the number 2.
    In two minutes I lost two dollars.

2. **there, their, they're**

    There means *in that place.*
    The supervisor stood there looking.

    Their is the possessive.
    Their paychecks arrived late.

    They're means *they are* (contraction).
    I hope they're not going to be late.

3. **its, it's**

    Its is the possessive.
    Our company takes care of its employees.

    It's means *it is* (contraction).
    It's good that you admitted your mistake.

Some other word pairs in the "must know" category are listed below. Look up the words and their meanings in the dictionary. Be sure to notice the differences in spelling.

your, you're	quiet, quite
who's, whose	than, then
accept, except	a, an
choose, chose	were, where
later, latter	of, off
lead, led	hear, here
loose, lose	new, knew
passed, past	

Here are some pairs of similar words you **SHOULD** know:

4. advice, advise

Advice is the noun.
  She gave me some good advice.

Advise is the verb.
  My boss advised me to take a spelling class.

5. affect, effect

Affect is almost always a verb; it means *to influence, alter,* or *change.*
  How will the new policy affect our benefits?

Effect is usually a noun; it means *result.*
  What effect has the incentive program had on sales?

6. brake, break

Brake means *to stop* or *a mechanism used to stop.*
  The brakes on my car are shot.

Break means *to split, crack, smash,* or *get rid of.*
  Can you break the smoking habit?

7. device, devise

Device is the noun.
   He installed an antitheft device.

Devise is the verb.
   I want you to devise a plan to solve the problem.

Here are some other pairs of similar words that you should know. Look them up in the dictionary.

alter, altar	decent, descent
angle, angel	desert, dessert
capital, capitol	dual, duel
close, clothes	forward, foreword
conscience, conscious	fourth, forth
council, counsel	whole, hole

Here are some words that you may have occasion to use in your writing:

8. instance, instants

Instance means *an example.*
   What happened was another instance of carelessness.

Instants means *moments in time.*
   The police were there in instants.

9. morale, moral

Morale means *attitude* or *spirit.*
   The morale of the clerical staff is low.

Moral means *good* and *honorable.*
   Mr. Bosworth insists on moral behavior among his employees.

10. **Personal** means *private.*
    I would like a day off to take care of some personal business.

    Personnel refers to *a group of workers.*
    All office personnel are required to dress appropriately.

11. **principal, principle**

    Principal stresses the idea of *main* or *chief.*
    My principal outside interest is photography.

    Principle means *rule, standard,* or *the idea behind.*
    The principle behind his investment policy is: ''Buy low and sell high.''

12. **stationary, stationery**

    Stationary means *without moving.*
    These parts rotate; the others are stationary.

    Stationery means *paper used for letters.*
    I ordered two reams of office stationery.

Look up the following word pairs in the dictionary. You may occasionally use them in your correspondence.

pail, pale	stake, steak
peace, piece	through, threw
role, roll	week, weak
shone, shown	weather, whether

There are dozens of other similar word pairs in English. Keep a notebook of confusing words that you encounter in your reading and conversations. These words **sound** the same, but they are different in spelling and meaning.

Also, review the section on apostrophes in Chapter 4. The spelling checker cannot distinguish between plurals and possessives. You will have to check this yourself when you write. Be sure you use the right word. When you mean ''more than one,'' use the word that ends in <u>s</u>. When you mean to show possession, use the word that ends with '<u>s</u> (only one) or <u>s</u>' (more than one).

Correct: The accountants all worked hard to meet the deadline.

Correct: The accountant's knees were shaking as he walked into the IRS office.

Underline the correctly spelled words in the following sentences.

Exercise #17—Spelling

1. (Its It's) your job to see that (there their they're) reports are turned in on time.

2. Who (choose chose) Sandy Potter to (lead led) the team?

3. I (passed past) along your (advise advice) and it seemed to have a good (affect effect).

4. How will the new (device devise) (affect effect) our January sales?

5. We must go (forward foreword) in this (instance instants) and do everything we can to ensure that the (moral morale) of the office (personnel personal) is improved.

6. I have (shone shown) him how to order (stationery stationary) and other supplies.

Correct Answers: 1. It's, their   2. chose, lead   3. passed, advice, effect 4. device, affect   5. forward, instance, morale, personnel   6. shown, stationery

---

Spelling Rules

You can save yourself time and trouble by learning a few spelling rules. By memorizing these rules, you can learn to spell dozens of words all at once rather than one at a time. The only problem with English spelling rules is that there are always exceptions. Study the list of exceptions provided, and then memorize them.

Rule #1—Noun Plurals

The plurals of most English nouns are formed simply by adding the letter s. If the noun already ends in an s-sound, add es.

> two computers
> four boxes

Exceptions: men, women; some words that end in y, o, and f; words that end in is.

> enemy/enemies   hero/heroes
> half/halves   crisis/crises

Rule #2—Final Silent e

If a letter isn't pronounced when a word is spoken, we say this letter is "silent." When a word ends in the letter e, and that letter is silent, follow this rule. To form a new word by adding a word part such as "ing" or "able," drop the e at the end of the word.

> use + ing = using   prove + able = provable

Notice that the word parts in this case begin with the letters i and a. These letters are vowels. **If the word part begins with a vowel, drop the e when you make it plural.**

Exceptions: words that end in ge and ce; certain words that need the e to avoid confusion with other words.

> courageous   dyeing (vs. dying)
> noticeable   singeing (vs. singing)

On the other hand, if a word part like "less" or "ment" is added to a word ending in a silent e, the e is **not** dropped.

> use + less = useless   excite + ment = excitement

These word parts do not begin with vowels. They begin with consonants. The letters l and m are consonants. **If the word part begins with a consonant, do not drop the e when you make it plural.**

Exceptions: argument, awful, ninth, truly, wholly, wisdom.

Rule #3—Write i Before e...

Most people who grew up speaking English know the jingle:

> Write i before e,
> Except after c
> Or when sounded like "ay"
> As in "neighbor" and "weigh."

This is a useful rule, because so many English words contain the two letter combination of either ie or ei.

The key to using the rule is to **hear** how these two letters are sounded when the word is spoken. If the letters are sounded like "ee," you should write ie or cei. **If the sound is "ee," write i before e except after c.**

| achieve | relief | yield |
| ceiling | receipt | receive |

If this two-letter combination is sounded like "ay," reverse the order. Write ei and cie.

| freight | weight |

The normal order (ie and cei) is also reversed if the letters have other sounds, for example, uh, ih, or eye.

| efficient | counterfeit | Fahrenheit |

Exceptions: neither, financier, weird, either, seize, leisure, caffeine, protein.

Rule #4—Doubling the Final Consonant

The doubling rule is complicated, but it is very useful because it applies to so many words and because there are very few exceptions.

Ready? Read these instructions carefully. You'll catch on quickly if you pay attention.

The rule is this:
If a word ends in a consonant preceded by a single vowel, double the consonant when adding a word part that begins with a vowel.

Word		Word Part	New Word
drop	+	ed	dropped
plan	+	ing	planning
big	+	er	bigger

Doubling also takes place in longer words—words of more than one syllable—if the accent (the part of the word that is emphasized when the word is spoken) is on the last syllable.

oMIT	+	ed	omitted
conFER	+	ing	conferring

If the word does not end in a consonant preceded by a single vowel or the word part does not begin with a vowel, do **not** double the consonant. If the accent is not on the last syllable of a longer word, do **not** double.

meet	+	ing	meeting
jump	+	ed	jumped
make	+	ing	making
fit	+	ness	fitness
FASten	+	ed	fastened

Confused? If not, you catch on very quickly! It takes most people awhile to learn this rule. Reread the directions and examples if you need to. Be sure you know what vowels and consonants are before you go any further.

Which are vowels and which are consonants? Circle the vowels.

e b j o u p l k a f r z i m y t d

You should have circled the following letters: e, o, u, a, i, and y. (Y is a vowel if it is pronounced ''ih'' as in symbol, a consonant if it is pronounced ''yeh'' as in yellow.)

Do you understand the rule? Take this test and find out. Assume that you are going to add a word part (ed, ing, er) to each listed word. Should you double the final letter of the word? Circle the word if the final letter should be doubled.

dream, grip, slim, write, blur, flash, wrap, fasten, surround, submit, refer, prefer, model, emit

You should have circled these words: grip, slim, blur, wrap, submit, refer, prefer, emit.

Why isn't the final letter doubled in the other words? Referring to the list again, underline letters that break the rule. Then compare your answers with those below.

dream	Two vowels before final consonant
write	Word doesn't end in a consonant
flash	Letter before final letter isn't a vowel
TRAVel	Accent not at end of word
surround	Letter before final letter isn't a vowel
MODel	Accent not at end of word

Now take a look at the following list. Why isn't the final letter doubled?

allot	+	ment	allotment
hot	+	ly	hotly
prefer	+	ence	preference
refer	+	ence	reference

Answers: ment and ly do not begin with vowels; when the new words "preference" and "reference" are formed, the accent shifts to the first syllable.

Do not be discouraged if you have trouble with this rule at first. Keep after it. It can save you a lot of time and trouble. When you have programed your brain to understand this rule, you will have a built-in "spelling checker" for more than 3,000 commonly used words!

Note: There are only a few exceptions to this rule. These exceptions are transferred, transferring, excellent, excellence.

Underline the correctly spelled words in the following exercise.

Exercise #18—Spelling

1. He (climbbed climbed) the ladder of success because of his (committment commitment) to (excellence excelence).

2. After (conferring confering) with the sales manager, we left for the (conferrence conference).

3. He (cancelled canceled) all his appointments so that he could spend the afternoon (digging diging) through the files.

4. I got a (sinkking sinking) feeling when I thought about how the competition has (robbed robed) us on the Acme deal.

5. It (occurred occured) to me yesterday that the stockroom is not (heatted heated) properly.

6. The employees feel that they have (benefitted benefited) from the noonhour (fittness fitness) walks.

Correct Answers: 1. climbed, commitment, excellence   2. conferring, conference   3. canceled, digging   4. sinking, robbed   5. occurred, heated   6. benefited, fitness

Test your editing skills. Circle the 10 spelling errors in the following letter.

Exercise #19—Spelling

1 We have an important announcement concerning you're ABC Insurance Trust group insurance.

2 The ABC Insurance Trust group insurance plans are now administered by Caspar M. Winters & Co., specialists in the union-sponsored group insurance feild for almost 30 years. Caspar M. Winters & Co. has had considerible experience in administering group insurance plans for unions.

3 This development assures the professional administration of your ABC insurance. Their will be no change in your coverage, premium rates, or insurance underwriter. The only change is with respect too the Insurance Administrator.

4 In the event you have any questions concernning your policy, please direct the inquiry to the group insurance administrator.

5 We are pleased that you have elected this valueable membership service and look foreword to continued service in the future.

6   Sincerly,

                        Stanley Larsen
                        President

Corrections: 1. your   2. sponsored, field, considerable   3. There, to 4. concerning   5. valuable, forward   6. Sincerely,

Train Yourself to Be a Good Speller

Here are some more things you can do if you are not a good speller.

1. Read more.

2. Notice combinations of letters in individual words.

3. Use the dictionary.

4. Take a class, read a book on spelling.

5. Use memory devices to remember how to spell words.

You can do many things to improve your spelling. Set aside more time for reading. You can't learn how to spell if you don't see words. Reading more will improve your other English skills as well.

Also, train yourself to *notice* words when you read. Some people seem to be born with the ability to spell well. Actually, no one is born with this talent. Good spellers notice words and combinations of letters in words. You can train yourself to have this same noticing ability. It is worth the effort. What do you notice about the following words? Look at them carefully.

absence	across
a lot	definitely
accommodate	separately

Many people incorrectly write ''abcense'' or ''absense'' for the word absence. Notice that there is one <u>s</u> and one <u>c</u> in this word, and the <u>s</u> comes first.

Notice that the expression *a lot* is two words. Look at *across* carefully and you will see that it has one <u>c</u> and two <u>s</u>'s. Notice that *definitely* has two <u>i</u>'s. Many writers incorrectly spell this word "definately." *Separately* has "a rat" in it. Many people make the mistake of spelling it "seperate."

Your spelling will also improve if you learn to use the dictionary. If you can't spell a word, look it up in the dictionary. Don't just copy down the correctly spelled word and let it go at that. Be prepared to spend a little time with the word. Read everything the dictionary says about it, including the meanings. Then **look** at the word. Then **say** it out loud. The dictionary will tell you how it should be pronounced. Then **write** out the word several times on a piece of paper. This process will fix the proper spelling of the word in your memory.

You can also take a class to improve your spelling. Many community colleges offer classes on spelling improvement. You can also ask a teacher or librarian to recommend a good spelling book.

Finally, use memory tricks to help you remember how to spell words. For example, you can:

1. Emphasize troublesome letters when you say a word out loud.
   sep<u>a</u>rate   Say "sep AY rate."

2. Find words within words.
   env<u>iron</u>ment pron<u>un</u>ciation

3. Use rhymes and other gimmicks.
   station<u>e</u>ry   station<u>e</u>ry means pap<u>e</u>r
   capit<u>o</u>l   the capitol building has an <u>o</u>-shaped dome

A poor speller doesn't get to be a good speller in a day. Don't expect instant success. Keep working at it. In the meantime, check your letters and memos carefully. If you are not sure how to spell a word, look it up in the dictionary.

CHAPTER 4—PUNCTUATION

Six Punctuation Marks

Punctuation marks are the traffic signals of writing. They flash signs to the reader: "Stop," "Pause," "Pay attention." Each little mark provides the reader with specific information.

You can easily learn how to punctuate correctly in a day or so—maybe in just a few hours. This book will explain the basic rules. Study them. Learn them one at a time. Then apply your knowledge in your own writing.

Begin your work on this building block by memorizing the proper use of six marks of punctuation.

1. Period

Periods are used to end sentences. They tell the reader to stop. They let the reader know that one sentence has been completed and another one is to follow. Periods are also used after most abbreviations.

> Mr. Smith told John to report early Friday.
> etc.   P.M.   sq. ft.   lbs.

2. Question Mark

Put a question (?) at the end of a sentence if you are asking a question or if you are quoting the exact words of a question asked by somebody else.

> May I take Friday off and work Saturday instead?
> Miller asked, "When can we expect the shipment?"

3. Exclamation Mark

Put an exclamation mark (!) after an expression that shows strong emotion. *Warning:* Don't overuse the exclamation mark. It is seldom necessary.

> Congratulations on your promotion!

4. Semicolon

Like the period, the semicolon tells the reader to stop. You can use semicolons to separate related sentences. It is probably better to use a period to end most sentences. Save the semicolon for separating "balanced" sentences, two sentences that are closely related in thought and worded in approximately the same way.

> I was sick on Monday; I was sick on Tuesday, too.

5. Colon

Use a colon (:) when a list or long quotation follows. A colon should always be used after a complete statement.

> I ordered the following items: paper clips, pencils, and felt-tipped pens.

> The speaker closed with a quotation from Mark Twain: "At seven cents a word, I never say 'metropolis' when I can get the same price for 'city.' "

6. Dash

Use a dash (—) to show a sudden change of thought or to emphasize what follows.

> Everyone will have to work very hard on this proposal—we must get the Bemis account.

Add needed punctuation marks to the sentences in the exercise that follows. You need to add more than one mark in some of the sentences.

Exercise #11—Punctuation Marks

1. Monday we got everyone together for a meeting sales reps, office staff, and managers.

2. It's a two-hour drive to St Paul we'll have to leave early in the morning.

3. Ajax sells the item for $7.99 we sell it for $8.50.

4. Have you ever been to Buffalo, N Y in the winter.

5. There's no doubt about it we are the best in the business.

6. The Fatburger is our biggest seller another top item is Calorie King Cola.

Correct Answers: 1. meeting: 2. St. Paul. We'll...   3. $7.99; we sell...
4. N.Y. ... winter?   5. it—we   6. seller. Another...

Commas

A punctuation mark that deserves special attention is the comma. The comma signals the reader to pause. If you say a sentence out loud, you can often hear a place in a sentence where a comma is necessary. It's safer, however, to learn the rules for correctly using the comma. People who punctuate by ear are sometimes wrong!

If the rules confuse you, try this: omit all commas from your writing. Study the rules one at a time. Then, when you feel that you understand each rule, try it out. Next time you write, keep the rule in mind and put in a few commas. Then learn another rule, apply it, and so on. Take it one step at a time.

Here are six rules for using the comma.

1. **Put a comma before <u>and</u>, <u>but</u>, <u>or</u>, <u>nor</u>, <u>for</u>, <u>so</u>, and <u>yet</u> when these words link two sentences.**

   > I was very impressed with his work, <u>and</u> I told him that he had a bright future with the company.

   Note: Do not automatically put a comma before words such as "and" or "but." Linking words have many uses. Use a comma before such words if the word joins two complete sentences.

No Comma:	Dick__and Sally will report in Tuesday.
No Comma:	I called him over__and told him to be more careful.
Comma:	Mr. Goldman called Monday, <u>and</u> he seemed very pleased with our work so far.

2. **Put a comma between items in a series.**

   > Joe, Maria, and Ted all signed up for the 401K plan last week.

   It's acceptable to omit the comma between the last two items of a series, but it's better to include the comma.

Acceptable:	My favorite sports are tennis, golf__and bowling.

3. Put a comma before an introductory expresion or an afterthought.

When you finish the letter, put it on my desk.

It was a useful meeting, I think.

4. Put commas around the name of a person spoken to.

I wanted to tell you, Linda, that you are doing a fine job.

5. Put commas around an expression that breaks the flow of the sentence.

Place commas around words or phrases such as *however, moreover, finally, therefore, of course, by the way, one the other hand, I am sure, I think* if they appear in the middle of a sentence.

I hope, of course, that you will decide to remain with the company.

Do not use a comma after the expressions listed above if they begin a sentence or separate two sentences.

Of course I hope that you will decide to remain with the company.

When words such as "however," "moreover," and so on, separate two sentences, put a semicolon before the word. You may also place a comma after the word. The comma is optional.

Most of the problems have been eliminated; however, a few difficulties remain.

6. Do not put commas around material that adds important information. Do use commas when the clause is not essential to the main sentence.

No Commas:	The man who found the error will explain what happened.
Commas:	Bill Wilson, who found the error, will explain what happened.

Note: Many writers are confused about the proper use of the words ''which'' and ''that'' when they precede clauses in a sentence. If the information in the clause is necessary to the meaning of the sentence, use ''that'' with no commas. If the information is simply interesting and informative but not necessary to understand the sentence, use ''which'' and put a comma before it.

Correct:	The policy <u>that</u> I outlined at Friday's meeting is now in effect.
Correct:	The no-smoking policy, which I outlined at Friday's meeting, is now in effect.

If you are confused by this last rule, you are not alone. It is difficult! Keep working at it. Remember: Use commas only around nonessential material.

Add necessary commas to the sentences in the following exercise. You may have to add more than one comma to some of the sentences. **Do not** add unneeded commas. Some of the sentences may be correct and need no additional marks of punctuation.

Exercise #12—Commas

1. A change in her attitude is necessary don't you think?

2. As I flew into Denver I thought up a new angle for the Las Parillas account.

3. Since I haven't worked for several years my typing skills are a little rusty.

4. Be sure to bring the charts tables and graphs to the meeting.

5. We wanted to have the party Friday but Mr. Simpson is going to be out of town.

6. The information that I sent you last week is incorrect.

**Correct Answers: 1. necessary, don't... 2. Denver, I... 3. years, my...
4. charts, tables, and graphs... 5. Friday, but... 6. (Okay)**

Apostrophes

Apostrophes (') have several important functions. They are used to show possession—the idea of ownership, belonging to, or attachment to. They are also used to mark missing letters in a contraction. A contraction is a shortened version of an expression; for example, ''don't,'' which means ''do not,'' is a contraction.

Apostrophes to show possession are used with nouns and pronouns. Keep in mind the fact that most plural nouns end in s, and they do require an apostrophe. We add apostrophes only to words that show possession or to shortened expressions.

Here are some rules that will help you decide when to use an apostrophe and where to place this punctuation mark.

1. **To show possession, add an apostrophe plus the letter s to all singular nouns.**

   The secretary's desk is cluttered.

   The boss's face turned beet red.

   Notice that we add an apostrophe and s to singular nouns even if the word already ends in an s.

   We also add an apostrophe plus s to a few plural nouns, words that do not end in s, such as ''women'' and ''men.'' Most plural nouns end in s, but there are some exceptions.

   The men's restroom will be closed for repairs Thursday from 1 to 3 P.M.

2. **Add an apostrophe only to most plural nouns.**

   The managers' reports were clear and informative.

3. **Add an apostrophe to certain kinds of pronouns.**

   Pronouns are words that take the place of nouns. They are used to give variety to sentences. There are two kinds of pronouns. One group requires an apostrophe to show possession or ownership.

It is <u>anybody's</u> guess who will win the football pool.

Another group of pronouns does not require apostrophes to show possession. They are already possessive. Do not add an apostrophe to such words.

<u>His</u> car is parked behind the office.

Here is a list of pronouns that are already possessive without an apostrophe. Remember, do **not** add apostrophes to these words.

my, mine	its
your, yours	our, ours
his	their, theirs
her, hers	whose

Confused? You may well be. The rules for using the apostrophe with pronouns are tricky. It's easy to confuse possessive pronouns with other words that do require an apostrophe. The words <u>its</u>, <u>their</u>, <u>whose</u>, and <u>your</u> cause the most trouble. They sound just like the contractions <u>it's</u>, <u>they're</u>, <u>who's</u>, and <u>you're</u>.

4. **Add an apostrophe to show where a letter is missing in a contraction.**

Contractions are shortened expressions used in informal writing. We can write ''That is not important,'' or ''That's not important.'' Contractions add a note of friendliness to a letter or memo; they make a communication seem more relaxed and natural. If your company has a policy against using contractions in writing that concerns company business, use the ''long form'' and avoid contractions.

If you do use contractions in your writing, be sure that you use them properly. Pay attention to where you place the apostrophe. It should go where the letter or letters have been omitted.

Wrong:	It does'nt matter to me.
Right:	It doesn't matter to me (the ''o'' in ''not'' is missing).

Here is a brief list of common contractions and what they mean.

isn't	is not	they've	they have
you've	you have	aren't	are not
don't	do not	can't	cannot
I'm	I am	don't	do not
I've	I have	doesn't	does not
you'll	you will	haven't	have not
she's	she is, she has	let's	let us
we're	we are	where's	where is
we'll	we will, we shall		

One contraction that doesn't follow the placement rule exactly is "won't." This word means "will not."

Pay special attention to the contractions *it's*, *they're*, *who's*, and *you're*. These words mean "it is," "they are," "who is," and "you are." Use them when you mean two words. Do not confuse these words with the possessive pronouns *its*, *their*, *whose*, and *your*.

Add the missing apostrophes to the sentences in the exercise that follows. Add one or more apostrophes to each sentence.

Exercise #13—Apostrophes

1. Ive been reading the bookkeepers proposal, and I agree with her suggestions.

2. The crew chiefs attitude hasnt been very good.

3. Its going to be interesting to see if well come out ahead on this.

4. The volunteers efforts were appreciated by all.

5. Dont take no for an answer; tell him hell never regret giving his business to us.

6. The stockrooms door is always open; cant we get some flypaper?

Correct Answers: 1. I've ... bookkeeper's   2. chief's ... hasn't   3. It's ... we'll   4. volunteers'   5. Don't ... he'll   6. stockroom's ... can't

---

Carefully read the letter in the following exercise. Add any necessary marks of punctuation. Do not add unnecessary punctuation. You will find 10 errors in the letter.

Exercise #14—Punctuation

Dear Tony,

1 Enclosed is your new personal property insurance policy. The premium has been paid as a credit from your old policy for the period of 02-25-89 to 02-25-90. There should be a cash credit from the old policy which will be mailed by the company direct to you.

2 I cant give you a quote on the auto yet because I dont have enough information. I have to have the exact make model and style of your car. I have enclosed some printouts to give you an idea. Also, I need to know how the auto will be used to get to and from work, during working hours, or just for pleasure. Finally have you had any moving violations or accidents in the past 36 months. After I receive this information the rest is easy.

3 I also enjoyed our conversation Tony. Not all that many fellow trout fishermen come through my office in a years time. It is always a pleasure when someone shares a common interest with me.

4 Please call me if you have any questions or if I may be of service.

        Thanks again,

        Mark

Correct Answers: 1. policy, which 2. can't don't make, model, and style used: to get Finally, have you past 36 months? information, the rest 3. conversation, Tony a year's time. 4. (no corrections)

In this chapter you have learned to use several important marks of punctuation. The third building block is now in place. Congratulations!

CHAPTER 5—MECHANICS

Capital Letters

Most beginning writers have to struggle to
get the first three building blocks into place.
But here's some good news. The fourth
building block is easy. It's a lightweight!
It takes awhile to learn to spell well and use
correct grammar. Punctuation, too, is a
matter of time and practice. But you can
easily learn the rules for capitalization and how to use quotation marks properly
in just a few hours.

Few words are capitalized in English. This chapter will tell you when to use
capital letters and when not to. Capitals are one form of alphabetical letters. There
are small-letter types and large-letter types.

Small letters:	a b c
Capitals:	A B C

Do **not** capitalize many words when you write, but be sure to capitalize when it is
required.

ALWAYS CAPITALIZE:

1. **The first word of a sentence**
   We will have Bill Jones meet you in Phoenix.

2. **The first word of a quotation**
   She said, ''We jogged two miles after work.''

3. **The first, last, and every important word in a title**
   I've been reading *The Business of Listening* by Diane Bone.

4. **Names of people, places, languages, races, and nationalities**
   James
   Mother
   Mexico
   English
   Asian

5. **Names of months, days of the week, holidays**
   <u>A</u>ugust
   <u>T</u>uesday
   <u>F</u>ourth of <u>J</u>uly
   <u>T</u>hanksgiving

6. **Names of particular people or things**
   <u>S</u>enator <u>W</u>ilson
   <u>H</u>udson <u>R</u>iver
   <u>M</u>ills <u>C</u>ollege
   <u>W</u>oodside <u>H</u>igh <u>S</u>chool

7. **Names of regions**
   the <u>M</u>idwest
   the <u>S</u>outh

8. **Names of specific classes**
   <u>M</u>ath 101
   <u>H</u>istory 17a

The general rule for capitalizing words is use a capital letter if a *specific* person, place, or thing is named. Otherwise do not. Most of the time this is easy enough. However, sometimes it is confusing. For example, the titles of relationships are capitalized when they are used as names, but not otherwise.

Correct:	Thank you, <u>M</u>other, for the advice.
Correct:	My <u>m</u>other corrected the errors in my resume.
Correct:	He talked with <u>U</u>ncle Charles about getting a job at the plant.
Correct:	His <u>u</u>ncle told him about the job.

If words such as ''my'' or ''his'' are used in front of the word, a capital is not used.

Next, let's look at some words that you should **not** capitalize.

NEVER CAPITALIZE:

1. Little words in titles, unless they begin the title

Writing with a Word Processor is a good book.

2. Names of seasons

<u>s</u>ummer   <u>w</u>inter

3. Titles of relatives when not used as names

my <u>m</u>other   her <u>u</u>ncle

4. Titles that describe but do not name a specific person

I talked to the <u>d</u>octor yesterday.

The <u>p</u>rofessor gave me a lot of help.

5. General names of places

The <u>r</u>iver is wide and deep.

I went to <u>h</u>igh <u>s</u>chool in Michigan.

6. Directions

The loading dock is located at the <u>w</u>est end of the building.

7. General names of courses of study

I am taking <u>m</u>ath and <u>h</u>istory classes at night.

Memorize these do's and don'ts and apply them to your writing. Remember that few words are capitalized in English. Don't capitalize a word unless you know a rule for it **or** you have some other good reason to do so. Even though there's no rule, you may want to capitalize certain names and titles. If certain words are ordinarily capitalized in the correspondence of your office or business, do what is customary.

Acceptable:	The <u>S</u>ales <u>M</u>anager will speak to us at the meeting Monday.
Acceptable:	All requests should be sent to the <u>P</u>urchasing <u>D</u>epartment.

Find the missing capital letters and correct the errors in the following exercise. Some sentences may contain more than one error.

Exercise #15—Capital Letters

1. Mr. jones always says, ''keep it simple.''

2. The senior consultant has written a book called *time management on the telephone.*

3. i was born in england, lived with friends in new york for a year, and then last summer I moved to oregon.

4. I have applied for a job in the admissions office of a local college.

5. maria is taking english and computer science at skyline college.

6. her doctor told her to take wednesday off and rest.

Correct Answers: 1. Jones...Keep   2. (Optional: Senior Consultant) Time Mangement...Telephone.   2. I...England...New York...Oregon. 4. (Optional: Admissions Office)   5. Maria...English...Skyline College. 6. Her...Wednesday.

Quotation Marks

Quotation marks ('') are used when you are reporting the words of a speaker. They are also placed around certain titles. You should put quotation marks around the exact words of a speaker, but not if you are putting the statement in your own words.

Correct:	Mr. Dicker said, ''I am very pleased with your progress.''
Correct:	Mr. Dicker said he was very pleased with my progress.

If the speaker says more than one sentence, use quotation marks only before and after the entire quotation.

> Ms. Haggard said, ''It is very important that you attend this workshop. If you do not go, your pay will be docked.''

Notice the placement of the marks of punctuation in the examples above. Periods and commas **always** go inside the quotation marks. Colons and semicolons go outside the quotation marks. Question marks and exclamation points can go inside or outside the quotation marks depending upon whether they are part of the quoted material or part of the sentence as a whole.

You should also place quotation marks around the names of

> **a story**
> **a newspaper or magazine article**
> **a TV or radio program**
> **a song**
> **any other** *short* **work**

In handwritten or typed material, you should *underline* the names of longer works, such as

> **books**
> **newspapers**
> **magazines**
> **movies**
> **a TV series**

In typeset material, such as this book, these names are in *italic*. Which of the following should be placed in quotation marks, and which should be underlined?

1. I read an article in Newsweek.

2. The article was titled, Smokers Have Rights, Too.

3. Have you seen the movie Wallstreet?

Answers: 1. Newsweek   2. ''Smokers...Too.''   3. Wallstreet

Punctuate the following sentences. Add needed quotation marks and place the other marks of punctuation (periods, commas, etc.) correctly. Underline titles of books and other longer works. Some of the sentences may be correct and need no changes.

Exercise #16—Quotation Marks

1. He said it would be no trouble for him to pick up the package on his way home from work.

2. The factory representative said, This assembly is all messed up.

3. I read an article in Forbes called How To Select a Mutual Fund.

4. Ninety percent of the friction of daily life is caused by tone of voice, said Arnold Bennett.

5. I enjoyed reading a book titled Stock Market Logic by Norman Fosback.

6. I said I would work Saturday, but I couldn't because of a family emergency.

**Correct Answers: 1. (Okay)   2. "This...up."   3. <u>Forbes</u>... "How...Fund."
4. "Ninety...voice,"   5. <u>Stock Market Logic</u>   6. (Okay)**

Format and Appearance of Letters and Memos

How your correspondence **looks** is just as important as what it says. Don't send out messy or carelessly corrected letters and memos. Be sure to use a standard format—that is, use proper margins, put the dates and names in the proper places, and so on. (See Chapter 7 for instructions on formatting a letter or memo.)

Here are some other suggestions for giving your business messages a pleasing appearance.

1. If possible, use a typewriter or word processor on a personal computer.

2. Never write business letters in longhand.

58

3. If you can't type or use a word processor, write memos neatly in longhand.

4. Do not send out typed letters with more than one or two errors corrected with opaquing fluid. Retype the letter instead.

5. Don't send out letters with errors in grammar, spelling, and so on. **Edit** your correspondence carefully.

Now let's see what you know about capital letters and quotation marks. Are the statements below true or false? Circle *T* if they are true, *F* if they are false.

REVIEW TEST

T F **1.** Always capitalize the last word of a sentence.

T F **2.** Capitalize the names of languages and nationalities.

T F **3.** Capitalize the names of seasons.

T F **4.** Capitalize the names of particular people or things.

T F **5.** Capitalize titles that do not name a specific person.

T F **6.** Do not capitalize directions.

T F **7.** Use quotation marks around statements that you put into your own words.

T F **8.** Place quotation marks around the titles of magazine articles.

T F **9.** Place quotation marks around the titles of any short work.

T F **10.** Underline the titles of books.

Correct Answers: 1. False 2. True 3. False 4. True 5. False 6. True 7. False 8. True 9. True 10. True

---

CHAPTER 6—STYLE

Developing Your Writing Skills

Congratulations. You have done a good job so far. You have studied the directions, worked the exercises, and begun to practice good fundamentals in your own writing. You have worked hard, and you have done the job right—building your writing skills from the ground up.

The foundation is now in place. Now what? Here's what I recommend:

1. Continue to work on basic skills.

2. Practice.

3. Learn the common style mistakes and how to avoid them.

It takes time and hard work to become effective at something as complex as language. If you have studied the material in this workbook, you probably know by now all that you need to know about punctuation and mechanics. But you will need to continue to study grammar and spelling. Don't worry if you still make grammar mistakes or misspell words occasionally. Give yourself credit for making progress. You'll be better as time goes on. Consider taking a course in grammar or spelling at an adult school or community college. Or get another book and study it. You'll find recommendations for other books on writing and basic English skills at the end of this book.

Continue to study and apply what you learn to your own writing. **Practice** is the key to developing writing ability. Write! Put your thoughts down on paper. When you have a finished message in front of you, go over it carefully, looking for errors. Put your knowledge into practice!

For now, your first priority ought to be developing your basic skills. Writing should be grammatically correct and mechanically sound. But good writing is not just a matter of grammar and mechanics. Good writers want their messages to be clear and readable as well as correct. They want to make a good impression. They want to please their readers and they want to please themselves.

Developing a pleasing writing *style* should be your next project. Work on the basics first. When you feel confident that you can put together a letter or memo that is grammatically correct and free of errors in spelling and punctuation, begin to consider other matters such as sentence length, word choice, and the order of sentence elements.

What Is Style?

Style refers to the characteristics of a person's writing. Some writers are relaxed, natural, and friendly. We get the sense of their personality from their writing. Their letters and memos are clear and easy to read. Other writers are stiff, phony, or cold. These messages seem to have been written by robots, not human beings. Some writers seem to be "putting on airs," trying to impress us with a foggy cloud of words that don't convey any clear meaning.

How to Write With Style

If you want to develop a pleasing writing style, here's what you should do. First, develop a brief list of goals. Then, each time you write, review these goals. Before you put a word down on paper, bring these goals to mind.

No one can tell you what these goals should be. That is up to the individual. One person may always aim for order and clarity when he or she writes. Someone else might value honesty and friendliness.

You will develop your own style goals in time. Until you do, here are three style recommendations. If you stick to this list, you can't go wrong. Remember, as you develop your own list, **keep it brief**. Don't try to do too much. Keep it simple.

1. Don't waste words.

2. Use simple sentences and familiar words.

3. Be sure the message is clear.

Economy, simplicity, and clarity are the keys to developing an effective writing style. Economy in writing means using no more words than you have to. You should spell out the details; you must tell your reader what he or she needs to know. But you shouldn't pad your sentences with unnecessary words. That's what economy means: making sure each sentence expresses your meaning in the fewest words possible.

Simplicity means using short, simple sentences made up of familiar words. Some writers use long, hard-to-follow sentences that are sprinkled with big words. They seem to feel that displaying a large vocabulary will impress their readers. Most readers are not impressed. Rather, they are suspicious, because the writing does not sound natural. Such writing is often unclear and hard to read. Good writers never try to hide behind a fog of language. They spell out things clearly in simple terms. They say ''hospital'' rather than ''medical facility,'' ''cheaper'' instead of ''with greater cost-effectiveness.'' Good writers keep most of their sentences **short** as well. They vary the length of their sentences, but they don't ramble on, either.

Above all, good writers try to be clear. How do you make messages clear? As a start, review goals one and two. If your writing is simple and economical, it is likely to be clear as well. Trim out unnecessary words from your sentences. Short sentences are usually clearer. (Twenty words or less is a good rule of thumb.) Use familiar words. The basic tools of the language also help to make writing clear. Check your letters and memos carefully for errors. Avoid grammar mistakes, incorrect or omitted marks of punctuation, and misspellings.

The Four Pitfalls of Business Writers

The most common faults found in business writing are listed below. Some writers are victims of all of these pitfalls, many of at least one or two.

1. Too many words.

2. Too many big words.

3. Backward sentences.

4. Clichés.

Let's look at examples of each of these problems.

Too Many Words

Many business writers are guilty of writing memos and letters that are unnecessarily long. Wordy writing is very common. The way to avoid this is to write the first draft in full; say what you have to say using as many words as it takes to say it. Then go back over what you have written, sentence by sentence, and take out unnecessary words.

For example, what can be cut out of the following sentence? How could we express the same idea in fewer words?

> **Somebody has said that words are a lot like inflated money—the more of them that you use, the less each one of them is worth.**

For one thing, we can strike out the unnecessary expression ''a lot.'' Also, does the writer need to say ''the more of them that you use''? Why not just ''the more you use''? Finally, the phrase ''one of them'' should be penciled out.

Here is the new sentence after we have trimmed it of unneeded words:

> **Somebody has said that words are like inflated money—the more you use, the less each is worth.**

Trim unnecessary words from the following sentences. Afterward, compare your sentences with the list of suggested corrections. Your cuts and the author's may differ. What's important is to express the idea fully and clearly without wasting words.

Exercise #20—Wordy Sentences

1. At this point in time, we should, or perhaps I should say we must, proceed to examine our policy of sales incentives.

2. I was unaware of the fact that your widget could be used for security purposes.

3. Mr. Jones, who is a member of the same firm, put the report together in a hasty manner.

4. The reason why we failed to reply is that we were not apprised of the fact until yesterday that somehow the report had been unavoidably delayed.

5. The fact that he had not succeeded was brought to my attention recently.

6. The degree of importance in the level of accuracy depends upon the individual situation.

Suggested Changes: 1. We must examine our sales incentives policy now. 2. I didn't know your widget could be used for security.   3. Mr. Jones, a member of the same firm, put the report together hastily.   4. We didn't reply because we learned only yesterday that the report had been delayed.   5. I recently learned that he had failed.   6. The importance of accuracy depends upon the situation.

Too Many Big Words

Another common fault of business writers is that of using big words to be impressive rather that simple, familiar words that send clear messages. Don't make your reader "translate" your communications in order to understand them. You don't have to have a large vocabulary to be a good writer. Plain and simple is usually best.

Can you put the following sentence into plain English?

Illumination is required to be extinguished on these premises after nightfall.

Wouldn't it be clearer to simply say, "Lights out after dark"?

Rewrite the sentences in the next exercise. Put the ideas in terms that everybody can understand.

Exercise #21—Inflated Language

1. My thinking has evolved to the significant point where a concept has emerged.
2. I acknowledge receipt of your letter and I beg to thank you.
3. Subsequently we will require your endorsement.
4. The biota exhibited a 100% mortality rate.
5. At this juncture of maturization...
6. Communication is the imparting of meaningful informational modes or concepts that impact on interpersonal inputs and interfacings.

Suggested Changes: 1. I had an idea.   2. Thank you for the letter.   3. Later we will need your signature.   4. All the fish died.   5. Now...   6. ? (This sentence is unreadable. I have no idea what the writer means!)

Backward Sentences

Language is a flexible tool, but sentences are most clear when their elements are arranged in a certain order. The main elements of an English sentence are the subject and the verb. The subject performs the action; the verb names the action. Clear sentences have the subject before the verb. When the performer of the action is left until later in the sentence, the result is a backward sentence. For example:

Backward: The <u>meeting</u> <u>was called</u> to order by Ted.
                        S   V

Better: <u>Ted</u> <u>called</u> the meeting to order.
                    S   V

Notice that in the first sentence, the subject of the sentence is the meeting. The meeting isn't doing anything—it's being done to. The second sentence is much easier to understand at first glance, because the doer and the action done are immediately clear.

Rewrite the sentences below. Put the subject before the verb. Name the doer of the action first.

Exercise #22—Backward Sentences

1. Plans for the conference will be made by the staff assistant.

2. An error has been discovered by our staff.

3. The report will be reviewed by us.

4. A decision was made to terminate the search.

5. The mistake in billing will be rectified by the supplier posthaste.

6. Receipt of your letter is acknowledged and appreciated.

Suggested Changes: 1. The staff assistant will plan the conference. 2. Our staff discovered an error. 3. We will review the report. 4. We decided to stop looking. 5. The supplier will correct the billing mistake immediately. 6. Thank you for your letter. (In this sentence, the subject—"I"—is understood.)

Clichés

Clichés are familiar and overused expressions. Business writing is filled with them. Here is a short list of typical clichés. How many times have you read these expressions in letters or memos?

> **enclosed please find**
> **please be advised that**
> **at your earliest convenience**

Don't patch your business communications together with outworn phrases. Try to find fresh words to express your ideas.

Rewrite the following clichés. Try to use simpler, clearer, better language.

Exercise #23—Clichés

1. Acknowledge receipt of

2. In reference to the above-named subject matter

3. Hoping to hear from you, I remain

4. As per our conversation

5. We are returning same herewith

6. It has come to our attention

**Suggested Changes: 1. received   2. (Omit)   3. (Omit)   4. as you said
5. we are returning (name item)   6. we have learned**

Economy, simplicity, and clarity are the style goals of a good writer. Good writers are honest, friendly, helpful—and they aren't afraid to show a sense of humor when the opportunity is right.

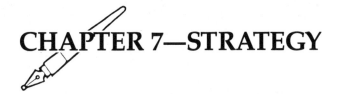

CHAPTER 7—STRATEGY

The Process of Writing

Get the directions straight, then **practice**. That's what you need to do to learn any skill. We've concentrated on the basics of writing in this book. Now it's time to consider the writing process and how to format documents.

How you approach a writing task is important. Next time you write a letter or memo, try this simple process:

1. **Think**

2. **Write**

3. **Check for errors**

4. **Rewrite**

Take your time and work out your first sentence carefully in your head. Everything follows from that first sentence. **Think** of what you want to say. Think of the words you will need to say it, and put them in order in your head. Then immediately put the words on paper. **Write** the first sentence. Then write the second sentence, and so on.

When you have finished writing, read what you have written. **Check** it carefully for errors. Ask yourself, ''Have I left out anything important? Have I included anything that isn't necessary?'' Then check each sentence to be sure that it is a sentence. Watch for incomplete and run-together sentences. Read the letter or memo backward (starting with the *last* sentence, not the first) if this will help. Then check it for grammar mistakes and errors in spelling and punctuation.

Finally, **rewrite** the memo or letter. All that remains is to put it in the mail!

Writing Memos

Now let's talk about strategy and format. Here are some suggestions that will help you approach a particular writing task—writing business memos—in the proper way.

- Say the most important things first.

- Make directives and requests specific.

- Use plain English.

- Set off important points.

- Keep memos short and to the point.

- Keep sentences short.

- Check for errors.

Getting off to a good start is important. When you sit down to write a memo, you have a specific reason for doing so. You have something important to communicate. Put this main thought down first. It may be a request, a complaint, an order, the answer to a question, or a word of praise. Whatever it is, this main thought should be spelled out at the beginning of the memo.

Be exact about what you want your reader to know or do. Make directives and requests specific. Say, ''Please call me on Monday,'' not ''Get back to me as soon as possible.''

Use plain, simple English. If your memo sounds dull and stiff, rewrite it in language that is more conversational. Remember that familiar words are best. Say ''use'' not ''utilize,'' ''begin'' not ''commence,'' ''end'' not ''terminate.''

Set off important points in a list with bullets (•), numbers, or letters. Notice that lists in this book are indented and either a bullet or a number is used to mark each item on the list.

Keep memos to one page **maximum**. No exceptions.

Keep sentences short; a good rule of thumb is to keep them shorter than 20 words.

Be sure to check your memo for errors. Your coworkers and customers will thank you for a carefully written message.

Memo Format

The **appearance** of your memo is important, too. Use the following guidelines.

1. Use the proper heading.

2. Start headings and each paragraph at the left margin.

3. Don't indent the first line of a paragraph.

4. Type or use a word processor or a personal computer.

The heading should say to whom the memo is being sent, who is sending it, and what the subject is. It should also give the date.

Memos should be typed "flush left." This means that the heading and all lines—including the first—in each paragraph begin at the left margin. Be sure to leave **margins** (white space) around the entire message—top and bottom, left and right.

Handwritten memos may be acceptable where you work, but it's better to use a typewriter or word processor. Write neatly in longhand (not all capitals) if you don't know how to type. Use a pen, not a pencil.

Here is a sample of a properly prepared memo.

TO: All Staff

FROM: Alma Martinez

SUBJECT: Linda Clancy

DATE: August 20, 1990

I want to let you know that Linda Clancy has started her disability leave sooner than we expected. Her last day in the office was August 13, 1990. In addition, Linda will be relocating to the Sacramento area following the birth of her baby and will work part-time in the Sacramento office.

We are still in the process of filling her position in the Personnel Department. In the meantime, all recruiting issues should be directed to Bob Smith at ext. 6378. All other problems should be directed to a member of the personnel department or to me.

Writing a Letter

Here is a checklist to guide you in preparing a business letter.

- Tell what the letter is about in the first paragraph.

- If you are answering a letter, refer to the date it was written.

- Be specific.

- Keep the letter short.

- For emphasis, <u>underline</u> important words.

- At the end, tell the reader exactly what you want him or her to do or what you are going to do.

- Close with something simple, like ''Sincerely.''

- Reread the letter and correct any errors.

A good business letter should be clear, direct, and businesslike. A letter should sound as if it were written by a human being, not a machine. Avoid business clichés and backward sentences. Avoid long, complex sentences filled with big words. Be positive, be nice, and be **natural**. Don't write, ''I acknowledge receipt of your letter and I beg to thank you.'' Instead write, ''Thank you for your letter.''

Don't waste your reader's time with long, wordy letters. Try to get everything down on one page. Rambling letters end up in the wastebasket. On the other hand, give your reader all the information he or she needs to know. Be specific. Include the facts, figures, and details needed to make the message clear.

Make your letters **look** appealing. Appearance is important. Type letters on good quality bond paper. Make sure that there are no typos, misspellings, or factual errors.

Always reread your letter before you send it out. Check it carefully for errors.

Letter Format

Here is a sample of a properly formated business letter:

WESTERN BANK
A Federal Savings Bank
931 Hillview Terrace
Fremont, CA 94593

May 16, 1990

Dear Customer:

Welcome to Western Bank. Your new loan has been placed on record and funds have been distributed. We are pleased to welcome you to our growing family of borrowers.

Enclosed is a brochure that explains how your loan payments are to be made. For questions regarding your loan, please write to the Loan Service Unit assigned to help you. An enclosure explains how to contact your Loan Service Unit.

Also enclosed is a card that outlines the benefits of our mortgage life and disability insurance program, which has the added convenience of including your monthly premium cost with your monthly mortgage payments. An authorized representative of Western Financial Corporation will call on you in the near future with more details about these and other benefits.

We thank you for your new loan with Western Bank and look forward to the privilege of serving you.

Sincerely,

Marie Harper
Loan Processor

A FINAL WORD

Many people give lip service to self-improvement. They are always *talking* about what they are going to do, but they never *do* it. Not you. You have tackled the problem head on. And you have done it the right way—beginning with the basics. Good for you!

Remember that building writing skills is a process that takes time. You're not going to snap your fingers and instantly become a good writer. Get the directions straight and then practice. **Write, write, write!**

If you studied this book carefully and worked each exercise, you have made a lot of progress. You have built the foundation.

Now you may want to go on and learn more. Taking an English class at a community college or adult school is a good idea. Or you may want to get another book and try a new approach or get more information.

There are several other good books in the Crisp Publications Fifty-Minute Book series. You can order these books by using the order sheet in the back of this book.

- *Clear Writing* **by Diana Bonet**

- *Better Business Writing* **by Susan Brock**

- *Writing Fitness* **by Jack Swenson**

NOTES

FOR OTHER FIFTY-MINUTE SELF-STUDY BOOKS
SEE THE BACK OF THIS BOOK.

NOTES

FOR OTHER FIFTY-MINUTE SELF-STUDY BOOKS
SEE THE BACK OF THIS BOOK.

NOTES

NOTES

FOR OTHER FIFTY-MINUTE SELF-STUDY BOOKS
SEE THE BACK OF THIS BOOK.

NOTES

FOR OTHER FIFTY-MINUTE SELF-STUDY BOOKS
SEE THE BACK OF THIS BOOK.

NOTES

FOR OTHER FIFTY-MINUTE SELF-STUDY BOOKS
SEE THE BACK OF THIS BOOK.

ABOUT THE FIFTY-MINUTE SERIES

We hope you enjoyed this book and found it valuable. If so, we have good news for you. This title is part of the best selling *FIFTY-MINUTE Series* of books. All *Series* books are similar in size and format, and identical in price. Several are supported with training videos. These are identified by the symbol **V** next to the title.

Since the first *FIFTY-MINUTE* book appeared in 1986, millions of copies have been sold worldwide. Each book was developed with the reader in mind. The result is a concise, high quality module written in a positive, readable self-study format.

FIFTY-MINUTE Books and Videos are available from your distributor. A free current catalog is available on request from Crisp Publications, Inc., 95 First Street, Los Altos, CA 94022.

Following is a complete list of *FIFTY-MINUTE Series* Books and Videos organized by general subject area.

Human Resources & Wellness (continued):

Communications & Creativity:

Customer Service/Sales Training:

TO ORDER BOOKS OR VIDEOS FROM THE FIFTY-MINUTE SERIES,
PLEASE CONTACT YOUR LOCAL DISTRIBUTOR OR CALL 1-800-442-7477
TO FIND A DISTRIBUTOR IN YOUR AREA.